ANNIE MILLER, a co-founder in 1
the Citizen's Basic Income Trust,
was also a co-founding member ѹ̣ ṭḥẹ basic income European/
Earth Network in 1986. She first became interested in Basic
Income (BI) as a direct result of her experience as a woman
of being treated as a second-class citizen by the UK's income
tax and social security systems. She is convinced that a full
BI, more than any other income maintenance system, can
help to bring about emancipation, wellbeing and justice. An
Honorary Research Fellow of Heriot-Watt University, she lives
in Edinburgh, Scotland.

Praise for *Essentials of Basic Income*

*This book is not really designed to persuade the unpersuaded of
the attractiveness of basic income... Instead, this book provides a
framework for activists that clarifies what a basic income is, what it is
not, what questions remain open for testing and where local discretion,
debate and detailed thinking are still required. It helps us get our
arguments straight and it stops us falling into some of the elephant
traps that are waiting for us.*

*One of the great strengths of this book... is that she provides a
very useful overview of all the different 'complexities' that are hidden
within this seemingly simple idea. Annie Miller's book provides
exactly the right balance of clarity and sophistication. For the
growing grassroots army, this booklet will strengthen our capacity to
make basic income seem both attractive and feasible.*—SIMON DUFFY,
WWW.CITIZEN-NETWORK.ORG

The very nature of work will change. The governments may have to consider stronger social safety nets and eventually Universal Basic Income.—ANTÓNIO GUTERRES, UN SECRETARY GENERAL, 25 SEPTEMBER 2018, AT THE GENERAL ASSEMBLY OF THE UN

This may be the time to consider a universal salary.
POPE FRANCIS, EASTER MONDAY, 13 APRIL 2020 [SEE PAGE 73]

[Some people] have suggested a minimum income, a guaranteed income for people. Is that worthy of attention now? Perhaps so.
NANCY PELOSI, SPEAKER OF THE UNITED STATES HOUSE OF REPRESENTATIVES

Universal income will be necessary over time if AI takes over most human jobs.
ELON MUSK, FOUNDER AND CEO OF SPACEX, CEO OF TESLA, INC., FOUNDER OF THE BORING COMPANY, CO-FOUNDER OF NEURALINK AND CO-FOUNDER OPENAI

By the same author:
A Basic Income Handbook, Luath Press 2017
A Basic Income Pocketbook, Luath Press 2020
Essentials of Basic Income, Luath Press 2020

All royalties generated from sales of this book will be donated to the Basic Income Earth Network (BIEN), Charity No. 1177066 www.basicincome.org.

The statements and opinions contained within this publication are solely those of the author, and do not necessarily express the views of any specific basic income organisation.

Basic Income
A Short Guide

ANNIE MILLER

Luath Press Limited
EDINBURGH
www.luath.co.uk

First published as *Essentials of Basic Income* 2020
This revised edition 2023

ISBN: 978-1-80425-092-1

Printed and bound by
Clays Ltd., Bungay

Typeset by Main Point Books, Edinburgh
in 10.5 point Sabon LT

Contents

Abbreviations

AI	artificial intelligence
BI	basic income
BIEN	Basic Income European/Earth Network
CT	cash transfers (benefits and financing)
GDP	gross domestic product
mdr	marginal deduction rate
MTB	means-tested benefit
OECD	Organisation for Economic Co-operation and Development
SA	social assistance system (mainly of income- and wealth-tested benefits)
SI	(contributory) social insurance
SP	social protection programme (cash benefits)
VAT	value added tax
UN	United Nations

Related concepts (Chapter 3)

BI + IT	separate BI and income tax systems
IT	income tax
NIT	negative income tax
BI-NIT	BI integrated with income tax system
non-BI	non-BI cash benefits
non-BI-NIT	non-BI cash benefits integrated with an income tax system

Aspects of costs (Chapter 7)

B	other cash benefits
PA	(income tax-free) personal allowance
TR	tax reliefs, (exemptions, tax loopholes)
ty	rate of tax on income
TY	revenue from taxes on income
Y	gross personal income

Introduction

GLOBAL INTEREST IN basic income (BI) has increased enormously in recent years, with the failure of many national social protection programmes and the successful BI experiments around the world fuelling speculation as to its worldwide applicability. A BI programme is not a policy objective, but an instrument which could result in a set of five simultaneous broad beneficial outcomes. The concept remains deceptively simple, however, and is difficult to define. The international educational charity, Basic Income Earth Network (BIEN), provides the first port of call for information about basic income.

Academic research and analysis provide the foundation in which advocacy should be rooted, thus helping to avoid false expectations, accusations of misrepresentation and political opportunism. The definition is the keystone of the structure. A clear definition enables more productive debate to take place, avoiding the confusion and frustration caused by talking at cross purposes, when people use the same term for different concepts.

The first task of this book is to propose an addition and some refinements to the most widely used definition of a BI. This is provided by BIEN on its website, accompanied by a commentary on the five characteristics that expand the idea, as revised at its General Assembly in 2016 (see www.basicincome.org/about-basic-income/).

The omission or alteration of one or more of BI's characteristics defines some related concepts, that are either already in common use or proposed in the literature. Special needs, such as those on account of people's disabilities, would be met via a separate system of benefits, in addition to their BIs.

Although a simple idea, a BI is a transformative instrument that could radically change many aspects of our lives. Its analysis draws on philosophy, ethics, political science, law, sociology, psychology, economics, environmental science and administration, among other subjects. For such a wide-ranging subject, it is difficult for many of us to create a framework within which to present a clear and logical development – which may change as one's understanding grows.

The second objective is to provide as clear, concise, accurate and comprehensive an account as possible, capturing the essentials of BI in a framework representing my current understanding of the subject. This book is intended both to serve as a reference manual for BI advocates worldwide, to make their task easier and to provide a tour through the basics for those new to the subject.

Academia and advocacy use different skills and voice and are complementary to each other. We need each other. A constant dialogue between the two groups is necessary so that the one can inform the other and the other can give feedback, for instance, about how academic language can influence, for good or ill, the work of BI advocates in persuading grassroots, opinion-formers and policymakers alike.

My third objective is that this book should not only inform but inspire and encourage others in the fight for a just, inclusive and compassionate society. The implementation of a BI will not negate all the economic injustices that so many of our fellow citizens encounter in their day-to-day lives, but it is a necessary step.

The effects of many of the (often man-made) crises that have afflicted the world in recent decades – gross inequalities in income and wealth as a result of globalisation, the power and domination of Big Tech companies and the Financial Crisis of 2008 coupled with austerity policies – could have been ameliorated by a BI.

The onset of the Covid-19 pandemic early in 2020 has presented the strongest case yet for the implementation of national BI programmes across the world, together with an international system to reduce global inequality and help poorer countries.

World problems have been further exacerbated by Russia's re-invasion of Ukraine in 2022 and its subsequent effects on both fuel supplies and grain exports to the rest of the world, leading to high inflation and the likelihood of a worldwide depression.

The fight for freedom, security and justice is more urgent now than ever.

'…individual,
unconditional,
universal happiness'

The Limitations of Social Insurance and Means-tested Social Assistance Systems

THE MODERN WELFARE state comprises public welfare services and a mainly cash-based social security system, which is divided into a contributory social insurance (SI) system and a mainly means-tested social assistance (SA) safety net. A BI would be part of the non-means-tested section of SA.

Contributory social insurance systems are inadequate as social protection mechanisms. They aim to provide *earnings replacements* for employees during times when they are unable to earn a living due to circumstances beyond their control, such as sickness, unemployment or retirement.

However, the coverage of a social insurance system will be incomplete because:

- it covers only people who are in paid work;
- the delivery unit is the individual employee;
- the amount of the insurance benefit is based on the

employee's contribution record;
- but, insurance benefits may be augmented to cover some of the employee's responsibilities towards his or her financial dependents.

Gaps in an employee's contribution record lead to reduced benefits. However, some 'economically inactive' people, including many (mainly women) unpaid carers of children, elders and others, are unable to build up their contribution records towards their own pensions, let alone receive unemployment or sickness benefits. Nor do self-employed people always enjoy the same protection as employees.

Social insurance systems work best for jurisdictions (nations, states or other authorities) with well-educated populations in a full employment economy, with state-funded childcare provision staffed by highly qualified nursery staff and where nearly everyone is in well-paid, full-time, secure employment over a lifetime.

Social assistance (SA), mainly in the form of means-tested benefits (MTBS), may be available for those who are not eligible for social insurance benefits. They are often below subsistence level.

Means-tested benefits are tax-exempt, but the system taxes the gross incomes of claimants twice inefficiently; first according to taxes on **gross income** and secondly according to a taper or withdrawal rate (see pp 21–22) creating a higher effective income tax rate for claimants than that faced by higher-income people, making the system regressive and divisive between net recipients and net taxpayers. By reducing net wage rates, it can also introduce an inherent disincentive to work for pay for lower-income families.

MTBs may be accompanied by intrusive **wealth testing** to identify saleable **assets** to be auctioned within the home, making abject poverty and humiliation a condition for eligibility.

MTBs are often subject to major structural faults:

1. The **benefit unit** could be a multi-generational household, or a cohabiting couple (married or otherwise), required to make a joint application for benefits. Thus, poorer partners may be trapped in the role of 'financial dependent', at risk of financial coercion or other economic abuse and with no independent source of income of their own with which to feed themselves and their children. They have no financial autonomy, power or agency.

2. SA benefits are **targeted** at low-income people, but do not necessarily protect them. Rather, it can segregate and stigmatise, humiliate and reject them, leading to a low take-up of the benefits to which they are entitled.

3. SA systems often **discriminate** between single people and cohabiting couples, requiring intrusive monitoring of personal relationships and denying married or otherwise-cohabiting couples the advantages of household economies of scale already enjoyed by two non-cohabiting adults

sharing accommodation. This could lead to the break-up of low-income families if the parents realised that they would receive more if they lived apart.

4. Receipt of their benefits is usually **conditional** on claimants fulfilling work tests and behavioural requirements. Non-compliance leads to sanctions and increases the risk of deeper debt or destitution, all of which creates stress and anxiety.

Thus, SA systems are often not only inefficient, misogynistic, stigmatising, divisive and punitive, but could also discourage claimants from working.

Fortunately, as enlightened jurisdictions begin to understand the negative effects of MTB systems, a BI can emerge like the sun in a new dawn.

2

Justification for and the Definition of Basic Income

THOMAS PAINE PROVIDED a **justification** for a BI when he argued that the land and natural resources belong to the people and where it has been appropriated for private use, those owners owe a ground rent to the whole excluded population. (Paine, *Agrarian Justice*, 1796).

Our economies are built on the infrastructure and material heritage of previous generations and who is to say whose forebears they were?

A 2005 World Bank study found that most of a nation's wealth derives from intangible capital, from human capital and the quality of its institutions, especially the rule of law. The wealthier the nation, the more this is so.

Thus, a BI can be **justified** as a dividend from the fruits of the economy, which is underpinned by these resources, heritage and institutions. An earlier name for this idea is 'social dividend', granting the same amount unconditionally to each and every one. Thus, no-one (not even a 'free rider', whose life is devoted to pure leisure) owes a duty of work in return.

BIEN's **definition of the generic BI** could be further refined and is also incomplete. It permits different amounts to be granted on account of such categories as gender, sexual preference, marital status, race or creed, or on account of any circumstances except for means or work. This is not consistent with the inclusive and liberating nature of BI's characteristics. A new characteristic, 'Uniform', which prevents casual prejudice, has close associations with both 'Universal' and 'Unconditional' and is positioned between them, becoming the new characteristic no. 5.

(Words in italics in this chapter have been changed from, or added to, the BIEN definition at www.basicincome.org/about-basic-income.)

A **basic income** is a periodic, *uniform,* cash payment unconditionally *granted* to all on an individual basis, without means test or *behavioural* requirement.

That is, basic income has the following *six* **characteristics:**

1. **Periodic:** it is paid at regular intervals (for example every month), not as a one-off grant.

2. **Cash payment:** it is paid in an appropriate medium of exchange, allowing those who receive it to decide what

they spend it on. It is not, therefore, paid either in kind (such as food or services) or in vouchers dedicated to a specific use.

3. **Individual**: it is paid on an individual basis – and not, for instance, *on the basis of a couple or* household.

4. **Universal**: *indicates who is eligible*. It is paid to all, *including children*, without means test.

5. *Uniform: the amount of a basic income is the same/ equal for everyone within a given jurisdiction at a given time and does not vary according to pre-existing categories or circumstances.*

6. **Unconditional**: *a basic income is not conditional on any behavioural requirements*. It is paid without a requirement to work *for pay* or to demonstrate willingness to work *for pay, to undertake volunteer work, or to behave according to traditional gender roles. In other words, it is **obligation-free**.*

The term 'basic' refers to the fact that it is a foundational income, or income floor, on which each can build with income from other sources.

'Without means test' implies the following:

- a BI is not allocated according to a person's pre-existing circumstances of income or wealth;
- a BI is *income tax-exempt* (represented as an intercept

on a disposable (or net) income axis, while *taxable income*, even for bands of *tax-free income* (taxed at zero tax rates), is measured on a 'gross income' axis);
- a BI is granted *prior* to taxation of gross income.

The definition of a BI is a concept based on its smallest common denominator of characteristics.
It is independent of and distinct from:

- policy objectives, including its amount (see Chapter 4);
- practical or pragmatic considerations concerning implementation (see Chapter 5);
- sources of finance (see Chapter 6).

3

Distinguishing Between BI and Related Concepts: Pathways to BI

BY OMITTING OR changing one or more of the six characteristics of the generic Basic Income set out in chapter 2, one can obtain the definitions of some related concepts that are either already in common use or proposed in the literature. Administrative differences may also reflect ideological differences.

Let us use a thought experiment to examine a system of periodic **income tax** (IT) payments, which, in this special case, is individual-based, universal and unconditional (without tax loopholes). It could almost be classed as a genuine BI, except that *its cash flow is in the opposite direction* to that of a BI's. Also, it is *non-uniform*, since the cash payments vary according to income. IT fails characteristics 4 and 5.

Next, let us explore the special case of a BI programme that is integrated with an individual-based, universal and unconditional income tax system, creating an individual-based, universal and unconditional **negative income tax** (NIT) system. The effects of the net cash payments of the resultant integrated BI-NIT can be very *divisive* between those people who are net recipients and those who are net taxpayers. The payments are also *non-uniform*. In other words, NIT also fails characteristics 4 and 5.

Few, if any, negative income tax systems are individual-based, universal and unconditional and not all of them are BI-NITs. For jurisdictions with a culture of paying income tax, an integrated BI-NIT could provide a method of introducing a BI.

Table 1: Six different combinations of BI or non-BI benefits and their associated sources of funding

Sources	BI	Non-BI
Integrated	BI-NIT	Non-BI-NIT
Separate	BI + IT	Non-BI + IT
Separate	BI + another source	Non-BI + another source

A separate BI program and income tax system, BI + IT, can offer some advantages compared with an integrated BI-NIT:

- Separate BI + IT systems can adopt different frequencies and timings for their payments.

- Separate BI + IT systems could guarantee a regular predictable source of income (that is, financial security) even if earnings and tax deductions are irregular and unpredictable.
- It will be easier to monitor whether the benefit system fulfils the BI characteristics if it is separate from the income tax system, which is often complex. Thus, a BI + IT system would be more transparent than its corresponding BI-NIT and therefore more accountable.

A **tax credit** system would allow the BI payment to be used to reduce an individual's tax liability, or even to exceed it, such that the net amount would be paid as a benefit. Similar to a negative income tax, it also fails characteristics 4 and 5.

A **means-tested benefit** (MTB) can be both income-tested and subject to wealth constraints. It is not defined by its characteristics, but by the method (a taper) used to ensure that a recipient does not profit unduly from it. A MTB is very much *integrated* within the income tax system. The gross incomes of recipients are double-taxed: firstly, according to general taxes on incomes after which the tax-exempt MTB is granted. Secondly, the joint disposable incomes of the recipients who comprise the benefit unit are further subjected to a taper or withdrawal rate, until the value of the benefit has effectively been withdrawn. The resultant high marginal deduction rate (mdr) can be calculated by adding the two sets of tax rates and subtracting their product. It leads to a very regressive and divisive effective tax system and reduces net wage rates, thus potentially introducing large inherent disincentives to work for pay for low-income people. This can be compounded by the practice of aggregating MTBs. The resultant cash payment is both targeted and *non-uniform*.

Ironically, the special case of an individual-based, universal in principle, uniform and unconditional MTB *at zero gross income* could appear to fulfil the BI criteria. But, being means-tested, that is, granted *after* taxation of gross income, MTB fails characteristic 4. Each can be represented on the disposable (net) income axis, the BI appearing below any income tax schedule, while the MTB is located above it but below the taper.

Neither NIT nor MTB systems provide financial security. The net payment due can vary. Its precise calculation relies on a continual flow of accurate, real-time information about the recipient's current levels of income from all sources, which can be difficult to achieve and maintain.

A **minimum income guarantee**, also known as a **guaranteed minimum income**, is a type of MTB where, if the disposable income of a recipient is below a designated minimum level, it is topped up to this minimum. Thus, in effect, the payment is being withdrawn at the rate of 100 per cent as gross income increases, creating both an *income ceiling* for those on the lowest incomes and an *income floor* for those on higher incomes. It fails characteristics 4 and 5.

A **categorical income** or **a targeted income** would be paid only to particular sections of the population according to pre-existing categories or circumstances. While a universal income could be either uniform or non-uniform, categorical or targeted incomes are automatically non-uniform with respect to the whole population. Thus, they fail characteristics 4 and 5.

A **participation income** could be similar to a BI, except that it imposes behavioural requirements, often involving paid or unpaid work conditions. It fails characteristic 6.

A **basic endowment** is a one-off grant paid to all, that could be delivered at the start of adult life, either as an alternative, or in addition, to BI. It fails characteristic 1.

4

Cases for Differentiation: Adequacy

THE MOST OBVIOUS case for differentiation is that for tax-exempt **disability benefits** to cover the extra costs incurred by disabled people (not just to live with dignity but in order to achieve their full potentials) which would be paid in a separate system to disabled people, those with chronic sickness and their paid carers, in addition to the BIS.

Jurisdictions covering a wide range of **climatic conditions** may need separate payments to protect those facing the harshest conditions.

If a BI were to contain a uniform element to cover **housing costs,** it would act as a powerful redistributive mechanism in favour of poorer areas within the jurisdiction. But it is likely to be the poorer communities in expensive areas who would have to uproot from their familiar neighbourhoods and social support networks, now coveted by richer people. In jurisdictions with great variation in house prices and rents, a separate system for meeting housing costs and related expenses may have to be retained or devised, in addition to adopting policies to stabilise prices and rents.

Differentiation according to regional price variations often merely exacerbates the situation.

The case for differentiated cash benefits could be met by a separate system of payments made in addition to the BIS, but sometimes it could be met more effectively and efficiently via public welfare services.

Cash-based social security payments and social services are complements to each other, rather than substitutes. Some needs are better satisfied via a cash payment providing choice – e.g. for food or clothing – while other needs can be satisfied more effectively by the provision of collective services, such as health care or education for all ages.

Adequacy

Differentiation could be based on 'adequacy'. Many aspire to a BI 'that is stable in size and frequency and high enough to be, in combination with other social services, part of a policy strategy to eliminate material poverty and enable the social and cultural participation of every individual' (www.basicincome.org/about-basic-income).

This may have been inspired by the Universal Declaration of Human Rights, adopted by the General Assembly of the United Nations on 10 December 1948. Article 25 (1) states (italics added):

Everyone has the right to a standard of living adequate for *the* health and well-being *of himself and of his family*, including food, clothing, housing and medical care and necessary social services and the right to security *in the event of unemployment, sickness, disability, widowhood, old age or other lack of livelihood in circumstances beyond his control* (www.un.org).

Sadly, as it stands, Article 25 (1) would not provide the right to a BI without the deletion of the words in italics above regarding patriarchy, circumstance and conditionality. Perhaps the UN could be persuaded to adopt the amended version?

Adequacy can be defined in terms of the fulfilment of human needs – implying that there is more than one type of need and thus more than one type of deprivation. Maslow's 'hierarchy of needs' is well-known.

Max-Neef claimed that fundamental human needs comprise an interrelated system; that they are finite, few and the same in all cultures and all historical periods. He listed nine: permanence (or subsistence), protection, affection, understanding, participation, leisure, creation, identity (or meaning) and freedom (Ekins (ed.) (1986) *The Living Economy*, RKP: 49–50).

Needs cannot be observed directly, only through the effects of their satisfiers, which are infinite in number and culturally determined. Cash payments are inputs in that they enable access to satisfiers.

'Absolute poverty' occurs when the satisfaction of human needs is insufficient for physical survival. Even with satisfaction well above this level, people could struggle to maintain good health.

'Adequacy' refers to the satisfaction of fundamental human needs to a higher level that enables behaviour to change and for the individual to thrive.

Adequacy, or poverty benchmarks, can be estimated in different ways:

1. Focus groups, comprising representatives of typical household configurations, are asked to agree on how much cash they would need at that date to achieve a particular standard of living.

2. Statistical methods that estimate the different parameters representing 'adequacy' or 'survival level' in cash terms, from the data of samples of people at a particular date.

3. Alternatively, a respected and authoritative institution can suggest a fair sharing of resources. The OECD's official adequacy benchmark is '60 per cent of median equivalised household disposable income for a couple' in each jurisdiction. 'Equivalisation' is the process of giving different weights to members of households to enable the incomes of different households to be compared.

These last two methods are based on the distribution of consumption or of incomes across the population. All three methods acknowledge that adequacy is likely to vary with age – for children, teenagers, working age adults and those of pension entitlement age.

So, what role could a uniform BI play in the fulfilment of an age-related adequacy policy? A BI that is adequate for the age group with the lowest level of perceived need could fulfil that same **baseline** level for the rest of the population. But the *extra needs* of the rest of the population would have to be met by 'topping up' with separate, individual-based, age-related, unconditional cash payments in addition to the BIs.

Pitfall for the unwary: take care to distinguish between the effects of a baseline BI and a lesser one (especially when predicting potential outcomes) to avoid false expectations or accusations of misrepresentation.

A baseline BI, together with 'adequacy top-up' payments, would cater for the general needs of the population, representing equalisation from the provider's viewpoint, based on sharing resources.

'Welfarism' is an alternative system that tailors cash payments to individual needs, representing equalisation from the recipient's viewpoint. It is not just some variation on BI. They are distinct concepts. Welfarism payments require their own definition and vocabulary. Implementation would involve a far more complex and subjective exercise, possibly requiring micromanagement. What is being equalised – utility (if interpersonal comparisons were possible), or a basket of satisfiers? Would individuals be compensated for social disadvantages (such as inadequate parents, childhood poverty, a poor education or a low IQ)?

A BI is a necessary condition for a fairer society, but by itself is not sufficient to bring it about. A BI is not a panacea for all ills. It also needs a range of other supportive government policies (such as equitable housing, a health-based drug addiction policy, social care, reduction in wealth inequality, carbon reducing measures and investment in infrastructure, technology and education) to fulfil a vision of a just, inclusive, peaceful society of fulfilled people.

5

Instruments for Change

WHILE THE ABSTRACT definition of the generic BI provides
a template for practical and pragmatic BI programmes, it is
important that it should remain both distinct and separate
from them.

The six characteristics of the generic BI define the structure
for a *class* of genuine BI models implemented within a wide
variety of cash-based social protection programmes, due to
the diverse contexts into which they would be introduced.

Context is important. Each jurisdiction faces different
opportunities, problems and constraints – presented by
(among other things) its climate, natural resources, history,
infrastructure, technology, institutions and culture.

A BI programme is a key foundational instrument, which,
together with other instruments, could form part of a
strategy to achieve a set of carefully specified and prioritised
welfare objectives, tailored to meet the needs of the
jurisdiction.

The cash transfer (CT) system comprises a cash-based social protection programme, flowing from jurisdiction to population, together with its sources of funding (which need equally careful planning) representing cash flows in the opposite direction.

The social protection programme could cover a range of instruments, including:

- The foundational, uniform BI
- Adequacy top-up payments
- Other differentiation benefits
- Targeted and non-uniform MTBS
- Retained social insurance benefits
- Other cash benefits for which a BI is not a good substitute, such as a welfare fund for emergency payments for fire or flood.

Decisions

Children's BIS will be administered on their behalf by the main care-giving parent or guardian. Each jurisdiction will have to decide at what age a young person becomes an adult and can administer his/her own BI. Should the BIS be paid weekly, fortnightly, four-weekly or calendar monthly, or could the recipient choose one of these?

In order to avoid possible economic disruption from its implementation all at once, should either a **sector** approach (to politically expedient children and seniors first) or a **gradual** increase of BI levels over time be adopted?

Practical preparations

Legal safeguards will be required to prevent later administrations from overturning a BI programme summarily. The individual's right to a BI should be guaranteed and not foreclosed on anyone who meets the 'universal' eligibility criteria, except by a jurisdiction's highest courts.

Protective legislation should prevent BIS from being used as security for loans and also ensure that a BI is inalienable, protected from sequestration (debt collection procedures), which otherwise could deprive recipients of their future income streams and put them at risk of permanent destitution.

A database containing the recipients' details will be required. Subsequent administration will involve: registration of births and deaths; links between parent and dependent child; changes in individuals' addresses and other contact details; delivery; and monitoring for continuing fulfilment of eligibility criteria, for fraud, including identity fraud; and for compliance.

All adults will have to set up individual (not joint) bank accounts. A child will need a joint account.

A register should be set up to record details of individuals with reduced mental capacity and of the responsible adults who will administer their BIS on their behalf.

Another register should be set up to record details of people with disabilities and the disability benefits to which they are entitled.

Adaptation of 'universality' to an existing situation

In practice, universality refers to the extent of a jurisdiction (that is, any authority with the legal powers both to implement and to finance a BI programme). The concept must be adapted into eligibility criteria. Since 'citizenship' is a multi-faceted concept, involving political, civil, social and economic rights and responsibilities, it could be challenging to apply. However, many BI advocates recommend that eligibility be based on residency qualifications, such as the legal right to permanent residence in the jurisdiction, together with his/her main residence being located in it and being subject to its taxation laws. It could include the fulfilment of a period of legal and physical residency prior to receipt of the BI and continuing physical residency for the major part of each year while receiving it, to support the economy of the jurisdiction.

The eligibility criteria will have to consider several categories of people, including homeless people, travellers, prisoners, nationals of the jurisdiction who have chosen to work and live abroad but now want to return home, students on exchange schemes, asylum seekers applying for refugee status and other migrants. Making adequate provision for those for whom the jurisdiction has no legal responsibility, including guest workers and uninvited migrants, is important in recognition of their human rights.

A worldwide BI system would be more effective than many current foreign aid methods for providing opportunities in poorer countries thus satisfying the aspirations of those who might otherwise reluctantly decide to migrate, adding to their countries' brain drains.

Integration of a new BI system into an existing benefit system

When a BI programme is introduced for the first time, thought must be given about how to integrate it with the existing **contributory social insurance** (SI) system. A BI should be able to contribute to many of the same functions for which SI was designed, as earnings replacements for employees during sickness, unemployment and retirement.

Would the BI be granted in addition to a recipient's existing SI pension entitlement, or would the latter be reduced by an amount equivalent to a lesser or equal BI? Certainly, voluntary state SI pensions to which recipients have elected to contribute (as opposed to mandatory state pensions) should be retained. Similarly, the portability of SI pensions for citizens residing overseas could also be preserved.

It is advisable to retain any existing **social assistance** (SA) benefits in place until the BI system is fully implemented, to ensure 'no detriment'; that is, no claimants being inadvertently made worse off as a result of the BI introduction. It is essential to protect the poorest people (those with no, low or variable earnings; who are unable to take on paid work: who are unemployable or unemployed, the old, sick and unpaid care-givers) from SA losses during this process, or better still, to improve their financial situations.

There are two ways in which a BI programme can be integrated with the existing SA system. Firstly, BIS could be granted in addition to the SA benefits. Some or all of the BI would be disregarded when entitlement to SAS is being calculated, thus ensuring that the poorest could be better off.

Secondly, the BIS could be 'bedded in' alongside the SA benefit system and taken into account when entitlement to means-tested benefits (MTBS) is being assessed. If the amount of a smaller BI increases in real terms over time, then the claimants would gradually be floated off the MTBS, allowing the need for them to decline naturally. The SA benefit system would gradually wither away, eventually leaving only a residual system of benefits for which a BI is not a good substitute. Both the number of claimants and the gross outlay on the SA benefits would be reduced. But it is only when the BI becomes greater than the existing MTBS that the poorest people would become better off financially.

New ways of accommodating the needs served by the residual benefits could be devised. A maternity benefit could be converted into a Child BI initiated at, or backdated to, the end of the first trimester of pregnancy. Similarly, bereavement benefits could take the form of the BI continuing to be paid into the estate of the deceased for a limited period after death to help with funeral costs.

Ironically, a jurisdiction with a well-developed social security system could find it more difficult to design a BI programme to fit in with its existing one, than those with more rudimentary ones.

A pitfall for the unwary: one should state only that the BI programme will be *integrated with* and not that it *replaces* the MTB system. The latter would imply that the MTBs could be *withdrawn* before the BIs are introduced and without ensuring that the BIs would be of sufficient amount to cover the MTB payments that they are supposed to be replacing. Talk of 'replacement' opens the door to political opportunism.

6

Sources of Finance

A BI PROGRAMME could be financed by either a single
source or a combination of sources. The source must offer
a reliable and stable revenue stream for the jurisdiction,
rather than one that is subject to cyclical or structural
changes.

Each of the various potential funding sources proposed
below has advantages and disadvantages.

A **wealth-holding tax,** such as a land value tax with
different rates for the various uses of land, could provide
a method of redistributing *wealth*, especially relevant in
countries with very unequal distributions of land- and
property-holding. If a jurisdiction kept a reliable register of
assets, then other types of wealth-holding could be taxed.

A **capital tax** on technology and equipment that displaces
labour would be an appropriate source of finance for a
BI. It would require international co-operation to enforce
it – as would the alternative of imposing dual public and

private ownership on the 'Big Tech' corporations in order to be able to distribute a *universal* dividend.

A progressive income tax to finance the BIS would be the most effective method of redistributing *income* from rich to poor people.

Corporation tax is a tax on the profits of companies and other enterprises. Competition between jurisdictions to offer the lowest rates of this tax to those corporations who register their businesses in their territories (thus reducing their tax liabilities) is leading to a race to the bottom and reducing the total revenue raised from this tax.

A **sales tax** and a **value added tax** (VAT) are taxes on expenditure (which, in the absence of an income tax, would allow personal savings to be free from taxation). The difference between the two taxes is that the VAT that has been paid by VAT-registered businesses can be reclaimed from the tax authorities, whereas a sales tax cannot be reclaimed. Expenditure taxes tend to be regressive and a dampener on investment and jobs. But a sales tax on goods and services, including those sold by international companies, might partially compensate for the loss of corporation tax revenue legally avoided by these companies.

The **Tobin Financial Transaction Tax** was proposed originally to reduce speculation in currency deals. It could be widened to cover other financial transactions but would probably require international co-operation to implement it. However, if each jurisdiction kept a reliable register of financial transactions it could charge a small rate of tax on each.

Taxes on the use of **scarce resources** and **harm taxes** (on the use of carbon, plastics and other pollutants, tobacco, alcohol, drugs and gambling for instance) are increasingly essential but are designed to change behaviour. When successful, these are likely to reduce the tax base and thus its revenue as a potential source of funding for a BI.

Sovereign Wealth Funds are based on community control of community-owned natural resources, such as land, water, clean air, oil and gas, minerals and other raw materials of the extractive industries, forests, broadcast spectrum, real estate or beaches. Their revenues can be ring-fenced for designated purposes. Alaska and Norway set up their funds in the 1970s based on oil revenues, which have been invested in the international stock market. They can help to protect intergenerational equity. Whether based on existing or windfall assets, they can be a long-term funding solution.

Seigniorage, or quantitative easing, refers to a government issuing extra currency to fund the BIs, thereby increasing the money supply. However, if carried out on a regular basis it would be inflationary unless the surplus money was extracted from the economy equally regularly via some form of taxation. In this case, seigniorage is just a temporary vehicle allowing the taxation stage to be deferred. Besides, seigniorage has a much more important role to play in financing both physical and social infrastructures, which add to the wealth of and therefore income for society.

Savings might also be made where existing benefit systems wither away, and fewer poverty-alleviation programs are needed. Or the BI eventually reduces the indirect costs of poverty on health and personal services and on the criminal justice system. Savings on administration costs could also occur.

Note: **Cryptocurrencies** are not currencies, but stocks. So, by what assets are these stocks secured and who controls them?

7

Costs, Illustrated with Income Tax

A PITFALL FOR the unwary: always indicate the context of the BI, whether a BI *programme*, or a BI *scheme* which includes a funding proposal. In this book, 'BI' refers to a BI programme.

The different costs of a BI programme should always be considered within the context of one of the systems of which they are part – the social protection programme, the income maintenance programme, or the wider cash transfer system.

The outlay, SP, on a social protection programme includes the BI costs, BI, and the costs of other cash benefits, B, plus the costs of their administration, A.

Gross cost: $SP = BI + B + A$

It is assumed for this exercise that both the BI and the other cash benefits are exempt from taxes on income.

Let Y denote the sum of gross personal incomes from all sources, of the individuals in a jurisdiction. This is the potential maximum income tax *base*, before benefits are received or taxes are deducted.

Many systems of taxes include a '**tax welfare**' (TW) programme, providing **legal tax avoidance** opportunities for many taxpayers, which reduces the tax base and increases the income tax rate for others who cannot avoid paying the taxes. These include the personal allowance (PA), (an initial band of tax-free income), together with exemptions and other tax reliefs (TR). These tax loopholes favour taxpayers, often granting income-tested benefits in proportion to their incomes, like a reverse means-testing system.

Let ty denote a representative *rate* of tax on incomes and let TY denote the *tax revenue* raised from all taxes on incomes.

$$TY = (Y - PA - TR).ty$$

(where $ty = 0$ for all $Y \le PA$)

The cost of the tax welfare programme, in terms of income tax revenue foregone, can be denoted by:

$$TW = (PA + TR).ty$$

The gross cost, IM, of the **income maintenance** system comprises both the gross outlay, SP, on the social protection programme and tax revenue foregone, TW, on account of the tax welfare system for the affluent.

Gross cost: $IM = SP + TW$

The **cash transfer** (CT) system comprises a social protection programme of outward-flowing cash payments to recipients and an inward-flowing set of tax payments to the state.

$$CT = SP - TY$$

$$= SP + TW - Y.ty$$

$$= \quad IM \quad - Y.ty$$

'$Y.ty$' denotes the **potential maximum income tax revenue** that can be obtained with the tax rate, ty.

The subscripts 'c' and 'p' below denote current and proposed systems respectively. (They could also represent actual systems at different times.)

Net costs play an important budgetary role. Three versions of net costs (NC) have been identified:

$$NC1 = IM_p - IM_c$$

$$NC2 = CT_p - CT_c$$

$$= (SP_p - TY_p) - (SP_c - TY_c)$$

A system where $NC2 = 0$ is referred to as 'revenue neutral'.

$$NC3 = CT = SP - TY$$

In the special case where $SP - TY = 0$, the **real cost** (RC) of a social protection system is the sum of direct taxes paid by net taxpayers and it should equal the sum of cash benefits received by net recipients plus administration costs. It is the amount of cash that changes hands and requires a computer-based microsimulation program to calculate it.

In this case, 'RC/Y' could give a measure of redistribution brought about by the social protection programme.

'Affordability', never defined, must surely express the fears of potential losers from the redistribution process in terms of percentage **net losses** and **marginal costs** (tax rates on their gross incomes).

Advocates in those jurisdictions that are averse to income tax should be able to develop a similar set of costs based on different sources of finance.

8

We Can Afford It: A Strategy

THE KEY TO a politically expedient cash transfer (CT) system is

- to provide adequate cash payments that could provide financial security, meet the needs of most individuals and reduce inequality; and
- to control costs to affordable, sustainable levels while retaining incentives to work for pay.

The following **strategy** could create a fair and affordable *income* tax system for funding the social protection programme.

a) Merge all taxes on personal incomes into a single tax in order to avoid favouring some sectors of society over others.

b) Subject all of each individual's gross personal incomes from all sources to this single income tax.

c) Subject the same level of gross income to the same tax rate for all individuals.

A basic income scheme compared with a typical income tax schedule

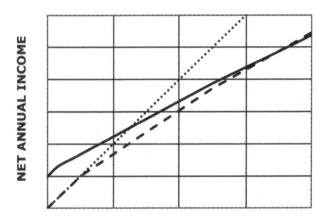

NET ANNUAL INCOME

GROSS ANNUAL INCOME

— — TAX SCHEDULE   ······· 45 degree line   ——— BASIC INCOME

The diagram shows the effects on net income of a BI programme and its associated income tax system compared with those of a typical income tax schedule. The BI is represented by the intercept on the vertical, net income axis.

Compared with the typical income tax schedule, the BI scheme provides greatest advantage for low-income people and this reduces as gross income increases, and is likely to become negative for high-income people.

The 45 degree line represents the effect on net income when there are no transfers or taxes.

46

d) **Eliminate all legal tax avoidance**: close all tax loopholes (tax reliefs, $TR = 0$) – *unless they can be proved to be in the public interest.*

e) **Thresholds**: retain a **small personal allowance** (PA), which could avoid tax returns having to be filed merely to declare small casual earnings.

These last two steps will make available for redistribution much of any previously discounted parts of the potential maximum income tax base.

Next, choose a higher threshold that is greater than the gross incomes of a large majority of adults.

f) **Income tax rates**: on incomes in the range of 0 to PA, the rate is zero, $ty = 0$; for the range between the personal allowance and the higher threshold, a proportional income tax (**a flat tax**) would be levied. This becomes the main marginal cost of the scheme.

A higher rate could be imposed on incomes greater than the higher threshold, especially if required to create a break-even point between the current and proposed systems. This design would effectively create a mildly progressive income tax system.

This strategy, compared with more progressive income tax systems, advantages the poorest while keeping the flat tax to a reasonable rate. It also ensures that the majority of the population are net gainers from the scheme and makes it more politically viable. A flat tax is inclusive.

g) It is more efficient for all social assistance cash benefits to be **exempt from taxes on income** (an intercept on the vertical, disposable income axis) rather than larger amounts being paid out and then taxed.

h) Deduct taxes on income at source wherever possible to avoid the build-up of liability at the end of the fiscal year.

i) Clamp down on **illegal tax evasion** which also imposes burdens on other taxpayers.

j) **Hypothecate (ring-fence)** the income tax revenue, TY, and use it exclusively for financing the cost, SP, of the cash-based social protection programme. This creates a closed, self-contained, income-redistributing cash transfer (CT) system, (that is, $CT = SP - TY = 0$), which merely transfers income from one set of people to another, and thus will not lead to a net (dead weight) loss on the economy. The distributive effects outweigh the overall cost.

Hypothecation also provides a method of **avoiding competition** for the same resources, between the income-redistributing cash transfer system and Government Expenditure (for indirect taxes for infrastructure and services, among other things). It also makes the income redistribution system more transparent and governments more accountable.

k) Administer the social protection programme and the income tax system separately.

l) Index the BI levels over time, as a proportion of either GDP per head or mean gross income per head, in order to reflect the prosperity of society and to protect BIs from sudden declines or erosion in real terms.

A BI scheme is not about some people giving up part of their 'self-made income' to pay for less fortunate individuals. It is about societies worldwide making restitution to the dispossessed, who have been denied access to resources and who live in poverty. It is about investment in the marginalised to enable them to transform their lives and develop to their full potentials.

Taxation is the price that we pay for a good society. Affordability is not about the size of the gross outlay or the level of income tax rates, but value for money for the outcomes achieved by the programme. This begs the question: can we afford *not* to implement a comprehensive BI programme?

9

What Difference Could a BI Make?

INPUTS AND SATISFIERS will include:

- both the structure and the amount of the BI;
- the structure and amount of other cash benefits;
- the structure, rates and reliefs in its funding source;
- the extent and quality of public welfare service provision;
- other supporting government policies; and
- the context presented by each jurisdiction.

The whole social protection programme and its sources of funding will contribute to the anticipated outcomes.

Each of the main defining **characteristics** of the generic BI could contribute directly to five related short-term and long-run simultaneous, beneficial outcomes/objectives for welfare reform. The **amount** of the BI and other cash payments will also directly influence emancipation, wellbeing and the type of society that evolves. Similarly, the **source** chosen to fund the BIs could have a direct effect on both income redistribution and on work incentive effects.

A **baseline BI,** together with 'adequacy top-up' payments, could lead to the following simultaneous beneficial outcomes, each comprising an initial financial effect, followed by behavioural changes:

a) **Emancipation:** a BI bestows dignity, privacy and financial autonomy. Each person is respected and valued for her/his own sake. By trusting adults with more control over the use of their own time, together with financial security, a BI emancipates and empowers them, increasing their life choices. No longer at other people's mercy, emancipation is worth far more than the monetary value of the BI.

b) **Wellbeing:** a BI can help to prevent, or at least reduce, both the depth and incidence of income poverty (in terms of material deprivation, insecurity, stigma and exclusion). Providing financial security – granting the unconditional right not to be destitute – could help to reduce anxiety and chronic stress and thus improve both mental and physical health. Enabling parents to spend more time nurturing and socialising their children would be an investment in the emotional and social development of future generations. In the long run, a BI could increase wellbeing, in terms of financial security, reduced personal debt, living standards, nutrition, health and educational opportunities, helping people to develop to their full potentials and reducing demands on health and other personal services.

c) **A just, united and inclusive society:** a BI could help to redistribute income, from rich to poor, men to women, geographically and over the life course. The flat rate of the BI would have a greater impact on those with no, low or fluctuating incomes than on those with high ones. Greater income equality would foster community and social solidarity and help to heal our divided societies. More choice over the use of one's own time could enable civic engagement and participation in public life. It could also enable participation in social and cultural life and lead to local energy and food self-provisioning. Eventually, it could help to create a just, united and inclusive society. But, *income* inequalities could be reduced most effectively if the BI system were to be financed by an *income tax* system.

d) **Labour market efficiency, flexibility and productivity**: economic theory recognises two factors that influence the number of hours in a given period that a worker wishes to offer in any particular job (her/his labour supply) – **unearned income**, including a BI and other cash benefits, and the **real net wage rate**. A BI will have the greatest effect on those who are deprived of either leisure or income (those whose labour supply is most elastic), potentially leading to a redistribution between those in paid and unpaid work, as people adjust their work/life balances. The reservation wage (below which it is not worth working for pay) can be shown to be a U-shaped function of unearned income, with a minimum at subsistence ('survival level' parameters in economics). It implies that individuals need to have benefited from enough endowments (such as a loving family providing a secure childhood, good health, good education, and/or current security, etc.) before they are able to contribute to society. Thus, a BI could make part-time work economically viable for unemployed low-wage earners. The ending of income-testing for benefit claimants restores the incentive to work for pay inherent in the net wage rate. A generous BI could enable employees to negotiate for fair pay, flexibility and good working conditions, or to refuse the worst jobs, depending on the labour market situation. A BI increases workplace democracy. More skills training and work choices could increase productivity.

e) **A relatively simple cash transfer administration system:** for individuals who fulfil the eligibility criteria, administration will involve registration, delivery, monitoring and compliance. Individualisation, universality, uniformity, and the non-conditionality of the BI programme would require relatively simple administration, reducing the risk of fraud or error by either recipient or staff, and keeping administration costs to a minimum. These characteristics should lead to less intrusive monitoring of poor people's lives. It should also avoid the time-consuming personal effort and stress required of many claimants in order to apply for and retain means-tested benefits. Eventually it could lead to a more transparent and accountable administration system.

Obviously, BI is not about just a single issue and the combination of community, equity, choice and efficiency outcomes appeal to those on both left and right of the political spectrum. BI's set of potential outcomes would appear to encompass *liberté*, *égalité* and *fraternité*. The defining characteristics of the generic BI and the broad outcomes to which they can contribute are interrelated. All of the main characteristics are necessary to enable both men and women to experience the outcomes. Even a less than baseline BI could contribute towards these objectives, given the poverty of millions of people living below subsistence levels in both rich and poor countries worldwide. The more generous the BI, the more fully will these objectives be achieved.

The underlying question for any policy proposal must be: 'What sort of society do we want to create for ourselves and for future generations?' One based on the ideals of wisdom, justice, compassion and integrity would appeal to many people.

Some institutions bring out the worst in people. Basic income seems to bring out the best. In the Indian experiment, the outcomes fell into three areas – an emancipatory effect, improvement in wellbeing and an increase in productivity. Some families, by pooling their BIS, were able to buy a family member out of bonded labour (Davala *et al*, 2015). Initial results in the Finnish experiment indicated that recipients felt much happier.

Adam Smith wrote in *The Wealth of Nations*, 1776, Book 1, Chapter 8, page 96:

Is this improvement in the circumstances of the lower rank of the people to be regarded as an advantage or as an inconvenience to the society? The answer seems at first sight abundantly plain. Servants, labourers and workmen of different kinds, make up the far greater part of every political society. But what improves the circumstances of the greater part can never be regarded as an inconveniency to the whole. No society can surely be flourishing and happy, of which the far greater part of the members are poor and miserable (www.adamsmith.org)

Who Would Benefit from an 'Adequate' BI?

WOMEN COMPRISE THE largest single group of people who would benefit from a BI, particularly married and other cohabiting women. They would be released immediately from the financial dependence that traps so many of them and with it the threat of economic coercion or other abuse.

Having their own unconditional source of income could emancipate and empower women. It could enable them to negotiate for a better allocation of domestic chores and caring responsibilities in the home. It could give them more control over major life choices, including leaving an abusive relationship, moving home, or taking a job. However, a BI is unlikely to lead to genuine sexual equality in society until the 'universal caregiver' ideal replaces the 'universal bread-winner' model.

Would a BI force women back into their kitchens? Many low- to medium-skilled, low-waged men and women survive precariously from day to day on a portfolio of insecure, soul-destroying drudge jobs carrying out essential work. They might prefer to spend more time at home caring for children, close friends, and especially ageing parents, a privilege that many wealthier women already enjoy. Both men and women face the same choice and it is the financial security of an adequate BI that could make that choice viable. Thus, it is the poor working conditions, not the BI, that would be 'forcing' them.

A BI scheme is likely to affect men's lives in many ways. Workers are aware that if they lost their jobs and were unable to find another one within two or three months, it could be followed by long-term unemployment, increased poverty, personal debt, the risk of losing their houses, marriages and families, and ultimately homelessness.

Financial security could reduce chronic stress and help to relieve other mental health symptoms. More men could have the option of choosing a congenial work/life balance and experience the joys and responsibilities of being involved in the daily care and upbringing of their children, or of caring for other family members without stigmatisation. Eventually, the 'universal caregiver' model, where all adults contribute both paid work and caregiving, thus achieving a better work/life balance, could also benefit men, thus leading to genuine gender equality.

A BI could provide the best opportunity for reducing child poverty worldwide. Young adults in their late teenage years and early twenties could also benefit from some financial independence, administering their own BIs and learning financial skills. 'Adequate' BIs could contribute towards their maintenance costs as students and help them later as young adults when starting out in life.

Writers, actors and other artists would value the security that a full BI could give them while developing their creative talents and setting up their own businesses. It could also enable people to update their work skills regularly and help life-long learning to become a reality for everyone.

Some Economic Effects of an 'Adequate' BI

A BI PROGRAMME would continue to provide an automatic stabilisation function for the macro-economy, as with existing benefit systems.

An 'adequate' BI, that is, the baseline BI together with an adequacy top-up payment, could help to regenerate areas of multiple deprivation. The people in these areas will have less debt and more money in their pockets; demand will increase; new companies will move in, investing in the local area and workforce, facilitating higher local and national multiplier effects. Those who are confident enough might set up their own businesses.

A BI will give self-employed people, small businesses and workers' co-operatives the necessary financial security to grow their enterprises, releasing creative energies. A population receiving an 'adequate' BI will not only make fewer demands on the health services but will also provide a healthier workforce for business, with fewer days lost to absenteeism.

Redistribution from rich to poor, benefiting a very large number of poor people, will give an initial boost to the national economy, since poorer people have a greater propensity to consume, compared with affluent people who tend to save more or spend on imported luxuries. However, policies to foster only *sustainable* growth will be necessary.

If the BI system were financed out of taxation, as opposed to increasing the money supply as in quantitative easing, then it is not expected to be inflationary. However, wage adjustments and price changes would still occur. Wage rates for unpleasant labour could rise, and those of interesting, comfortable jobs are likely to fall. If the supply of a particular good (such as affordable housing) did not rise to meet increased demand, then its price could rise in the short term.

Eventually, an 'adequate' BI could lead to a lower national minimum wage. Employers might reduce their standard working week, or their wage rates (as will their competitors, competing away excess profits) enabling companies to trade more successfully.

Automation and artificial intelligence (AI) have already made a profound impact on labour forces around the world, replacing many unskilled and low-skilled jobs. The number of workers in low-waged, part-time, precarious jobs is increasing. Many former middle managers are now having to compete in this gig economy. Nor have the professional classes emerged unscathed.

It is still unknown whether this automation revolution will continue at the same pace or how long it will take for the promised replacement jobs to appear, or what quality of jobs they will be. It could lead to further inequality through divisions into high- and low-paid workers. Automation and AI are more likely to threaten workers' rights and solidarity than a BI. But compared with means-tested benefits, a BI programme would provide better protection for the population in the event of loss of jobs due to either further automation or the recurrence of a recession, or a depression.

A lesser BI would not be enough to live on, so there would certainly be financial incentives to work for pay. Even with an 'adequate' BI, people would still want to earn and spend or save more.

In addition to the financial incentives described on pp 52–53, there are non-financial incentives to work for pay such as the social and health advantages that employment offers – the chance to make friends, to have a structure to one's day or week, to develop one's skills, to take pride in carrying out socially useful work well, to be acknowledged as someone who is contributing to society, and general job satisfaction.

Some might prefer to use their BIs to pursue educational goals. Others might want to take an occasional sabbatical to travel or to achieve some lifetime ambition.

Since a BI would enable people to have more choice over the use of their own time, there could be an increase in working on one's own account, such as learning crafts or growing one's own food and selling the surplus. There could be an expansion of true craftsmanship leading to luxury goods that are preferred to robot-designed and created products. Growth in the education, care (especially elder care), health maintenance, creative and leisure industries would be likely. A BI would give financial security to those working precariously in the retail, entertainment, hospitality and other similar industries. People would make new social alliances for volunteer services and community work.

While not necessarily having a direct effect on environmental issues, decoupling income from paid work could give concerned individuals more time to reflect and to act appropriately. Localisation could reduce both commuting and transport emissions.

Current policies tend to focus on economic growth (and occasionally even *sustainable* growth). However, in the future, this focus must change towards *de-growth*, that is, reducing total material output in order to conserve the earth's resources and reduce pollution. Might people even have to be discouraged from working? The system for the distribution of the output of the jurisdiction will be even more important in these circumstances than currently. Having a BI in place well before de-growth becomes formal policy could ease this process enormously.

A BI programme is an act of investment in the people as part of society's infrastructure, underpinned by compassion, our humanity, and the recognition of our interdependence and thus our mutual responsibility for each other. The right to life, and not to be destitute nor to die prematurely from the 'crime' of being poor, should be sacrosanct. It is not a form of charity or welfare, but is about justice, with the emphasis on prevention, rather than cure.

Valid criticism of BI

THERE ARE TWO main types of arguments in philosophy:

- Normative statements are value based; for example, 'everyone should be made to work'.
- Positive arguments are ones that could be tested empirically, such as, 'total labour supply hours would decrease on the introduction of BI'.

Normative arguments

'Normative' arguments are basically statements of preference. Expression of a preference between alternatives is not necessarily a criticism of the rejected option. Nor can criticisms of a particular BI programme or scheme, even if justified, necessarily be taken as criticisms of the generic BI. So, what constitutes valid criticism and what is merely a difference of preferences?

An example of a normative statement would be the acceptance or otherwise of the BI's characteristics or its outcomes.

Some people dislike the fact that married and other cohabiting couples would gain the advantages of household economies of scale as a result of an individual-based and uniform BI, which two non-cohabiting adults sharing accommodation might already enjoy. Household economies of scale provide an incentive for people to share accommodation (including the parents of dependent children who want to stay together) reducing the demand for single-adult housing.

Some people object to giving BIs to rich people (who do not need the money) in spite of the efficiency of BIs compared with means-tested benefits. BIs are necessary in order to create a just, united and *inclusive* society. Affluent people tend to value universal systems from which they benefit and thus protect them more effectively for society's most vulnerable, compared with targeted systems.

Others reject what they perceive as 'giving something for nothing in return' aspect of an unconditional BI, leading to free-riders (whose lives are devoted to pure leisure) and other 'lazy scoundrels' (as named by the popular press). They demand reciprocity, extracting first (even from people who have nothing) before giving anything. Yet, Paine's justification indicates that a BI is a right and so nothing should be claimed from anyone, including free-riders.

Ideological differences provide normative arguments. BI advocates and 'labourists' (for whom 'work is what gives meaning to life') share some common objectives but the latter give primacy to work for pay, advantaging workers

over the many 'economically inactive' people who are
unable to compete in the labour market. They also often
recommend the provision of job guarantees, and a system
of couple- or household-based, conditional, income-tested
guaranteed minimum incomes.

In contrast, neoliberals appear to aspire to low taxation,
minimal government and a market-driven economy,
for a society of self-reliant individuals oblivious to the
interdependence between human beings (and thus to their
mutual responsibility) and who appear to be devoid of
empathy. Some neoliberals could accept a BI system in
exchange for the dismantling of all public welfare services.

Positive arguments

Positive criticism starts with an examination of the validity
of assumptions about behaviour, and of the impeccability of
the logic applied.

It would be valid to expose any flaws discovered in the
logic leading to both the outcomes claimed for BIs, and
the mechanisms identified as the means by which they are
brought about. Proof that *exactly the same* outcomes could
be achieved more efficiently or effectively by some other
method would certainly be valid.

Typical questions for empirical testing are:

- Are the assumptions about the behavioural responses
  borne out by evidence?

- Will a BI programme really lead to the outcomes claimed for it, especially those about reduction of poverty and inequality?
- What are the gross and net costs of a particular BI scheme?
- Will the work incentive effects of a particular BI scheme lead to an increase or a decrease in labour supply or to large numbers of free-riders? Empirical results so far have found that most people do not want to make major reductions in their hours of paid work.
- Would a particular BI scheme lead to a decrease in economic growth rates, or even to a negative growth rate and thence a downward spiral of the economy?

Obviously, there is potential for more research to be carried out in these areas.

Critics can also be expected to be:

- resistant to change;
- wary of unanticipated consequences;
- sceptical about administrative competence;
- mistrustful of politicians' intentions and aware of the roadblocks in the political process.
- doubtful about BI – as less of an opportunity, perhaps, and more of a risk, suspecting high costs in the event of failure.

Institutions and individuals who anticipate losses – power, prestige and influence, or of their jobs and other personal income or wealth – will raise their voices loudly against a BI. Loss of face is painful.

Discussions with critics of BI provide an important opportunity for well-prepared BI advocates and an informed public to rehearse the counter arguments.

Some of the most troublesome critics argue from the advantage point of complete ignorance about the BI idea and its ramifications, raising all sorts of straw men to be shot down. Those critics who have done their homework, putting in the time to study the subject so that they at least know what they are talking about, deserve our respect, even if not our agreement.

13

Evidence from Around the World

AT THE FIRST BIEN conference in Louvain-La-Neuve,
Belgium in September 1986, many delegates presented
theoretical research papers. Over the years, their depth
and range has increased. They have become accompanied
by computer-based, microsimulation thought experiments
and by theoretical papers advising how to conduct BI pilot
experiments. Latterly, more empirical evidence from BI
projects has become available.

Both taxation and benefit microsimulation (TBM) analyses and
BI pilot projects are methods of generating databases that can
subsequently be examined, using standard statistical and other
techniques. Each starts with a sample of subjects, which will
typically provide social characteristics and demographic data.
Each method has its strengths and limitations. Neither can
predict the long-term effects of BI systems.

TBM analysis comes logically prior to pilot projects, because
it explores the immediate financial effects of proposed
taxation and benefit changes on the disposable incomes

of individuals or households in the population sample. It can calculate gains and losses, identify who is affected, and how many. It can calculate reductions in poverty, the gross and other costs of BI schemes and the values of inequality measures before and after the changes.

On the other hand, TBM analysis cannot predict changes in attitudes or behavioural responses, such as how people will change the use of their time, or their consumption and savings patterns, or their life events as a result of the benefit and tax changes. The costs of setting up and regularly updating a microsimulation model are not cheap, but they are much cheaper than pilot projects.

Several pilot projects based on BI or related concepts have been conducted over the last half century, with interesting results that give indications of attitudinal changes and behavioural responses in a variety of circumstances. They are not capable of predicting overall redistribution effects, and there can be ethical implications.

They tend to be expensive, long-term projects, lasting as long as 6–7 years from the initial planning to the final stage. The stages would cover:

- specifying the objectives of the project – educational goals, testing hypotheses about BIs, and demonstrating administrative and economic viability in practice;
- the design of the experiment – the BI programme and finance method proposed, sample sizes for subjects and control groups, designing questionnaires;

- estimating costs and securing the funds;
- preparing the sample population and controls;
- 2–3 years duration;
- another year or more of collating results, analysing the data generated and evaluation; and
- finally writing up and disseminating the results.

The first of such projects took place in North America: the four Negative Income Tax experiments in the USA between 1968 and 1980; the Mincome Experiment in Dauphin, Manitoba, Canada, 1974–79; and the Alaska Permanent Fund Dividend, 1982–present. Then the focus shifted to Africa and Asia with the project in the rural settlement of Otjivero-Omitara in Namibia, 2008–09; Macau's annual state bonus as part of its Wealth Partaking Scheme based on gaming profits, 2008–present; Iran, 2010–16; Madhya Pradesh, India, 2011–13; Gyeonggi Province in South Korea, 2019–20. The BI projects arrived only lately to Europe: Finland, 2017–18.

Other projects have finished, started, or are being planned: in the Netherlands; in Barcelona, Spain; in California, USA, by the Y-Combinator company; in Uganda and Kenya (financed privately by charities) and in several mayoral cities in the USA. Details can be found by searching by country on the BIEN website (www.basicincome.org).

Other research projects use labour supply models to study work incentive effects, and the effects of poverty and inequality on physical and mental health and on the life chances of children.

Many BI advocates are confident that sufficient information is already available to enable the effects of BI schemes to be predicted. A carefully planned, nationwide, low-BI programme could be safely introduced and could be simpler to design and implement than a comparable BI experiment.

14

Where Next?

WE LIVE IN times of great uncertainty. Extreme problems (mainly man-made) face the world, of which the most urgent and severe is still the environmental threat of the climate emergency and species extinction. An 'adequate' BI could help to tackle poverty and inequality and give people more financial security and choice in their lives.

However, the urgency of these crises has been overtaken by the outbreak of Covid-19 early in 2020. Never has there been a stronger case for a basic income than this pandemic. If BI systems had already been in place in nations across the world, their populations would have suffered far less anxiety about their subsistence and experienced financial security during the lockdowns.

The virus has exposed the enormous holes in social protection 'safety *nots*' around the world. Numerous BIEN-affiliated groups and others have petitioned their governments asking for the immediate implementation of emergency BI schemes during and after the pandemic. Governments have responded with a variety of welcome measures but few, if any so far, would be recognised as genuine BIS.

On Easter Monday, 13 April 2020, Pope Francis stated: *'Tal vez sea tiempo de pensar en un salario universal…'*

As reported by Oxfam on 15 April, this was in the following context:

> Many of you live from day to day, without any type of legal guarantee to protect you. Street vendors, recyclers, carnies, small farmers, construction workers, dressmakers, the different kinds of caregivers: you who are informal, working on your own or in the grassroots economy, you who have no steady income to get you through this hard time… and the lockdowns are becoming unbearable. This may be the time to consider a universal basic wage which would acknowledge and dignify the noble, essential tasks you carry out. It would ensure and concretely achieve the ideal, at once so human and so Christian, of no worker without rights (www.oxfamblogs.org).

A letter, signed by many BI groups, has been sent to António Guterres, UN Secretary General, urging him to invite discussion of and endorsement for basic income in the United Nations.

The first duty of each government during the pandemic is to save lives and to minimise the adverse effects of the virus on the physical and mental health of the people.

The second duty must be the security of its population, that is the *income security* of all, providing enough to prevent poverty and for people to feel financially secure. Workers with mild symptoms would not have to choose between staying at home or going to work for an income to buy food and pay the rent. A BI could have reduced the speed of the spread of the virus. It would have been a public good helping to protect everyone across the globe as well as nationally.

Thirdly, a government must reduce the risk of recession or depression resulting from the reduced spending power of redundant employees and self-employed people. A BI could have maintained income in people's pockets and thus the demand for goods that satisfy basic needs. Fewer workers might have been made redundant, and fewer businesses would have been lost. There could have been more surviving companies to pick up renewed demand after the pandemic.

The world has been changed by the pandemic. We have the opportunity to rethink our priorities. We do not have to return to a business-as-usual, self-serving, exploitative, cruel world. The fact that people do care about their neighbours, amply demonstrated even to the extent of putting their lives at risk for them, can be harnessed to create a more compassionate, just world. It could provide the opportunity to reduce carbon emissions and reverse climate change.

Even before the pandemic had subsided, Russia's

re-invasion of Ukraine started its devastating destruction locally and has also led to worldwide shortages of fuel, minerals and different types of grains, with their resultant inflationary price increases. The potential threat of widespread famines, a depression and the possibly of war elsewhere hang over the world and, once again, it will be the poorest and most vulnerable who are likely to suffer most.

BI programmes can play important roles as peace-building projects, reconciling and healing divided societies.

Now is the time of the activist, whose task is to use skills and voice to translate the facts, figures and empirical evidence produced by researchers and other academics into narratives and personal stories; to change world views about what is and what could be and thus to change hearts and minds at grassroots level, of opinion-formers and policymakers. Although redistributive policies have occasionally emanated from above, a clamour for change by a mass of well-informed voters engaging with their elected representatives and briefing them about BI, supported by evidence so that the representatives can speak confidently on their behalf, would be a much more reliable route.

If a few countries were to implement BI schemes, and their beneficial effects flourished for all to see, it might be followed by a wave of national BI schemes being adopted across the earth relatively quickly. The next step could be a worldwide BI scheme alongside the national ones, which could help poorer countries and bring about world justice.

A basic income is not sufficient on its own for a better society, but it is a necessary condition. It could bring out the best in people and change societies of fear and despair into ones of compassion, justice, trust and hope. It could lead to new relationships between society, the state and its citizens. It could transform societies into ones where everyone matters and all can flourish – a veritable velvet revolution indeed.

Select Bibliography

Bregman, Rutger, *Utopia for Realists: And How We Can Get There*, London: Bloomsbury, 2017

Davala, Sarath, Jhabvala, Renana, Kapoor Mehta, Soumya and Standing, Guy, *Basic Income: A Transformative Policy for India*, London: Bloomsbury, 2015

Standing, Guy, *Basic Income: And How We Can Make It Happen*, Basingstoke: Pelican, 2017

Torry, Malcolm, *Why We Need a Citizen's Basic Income: The Desirability, Feasibility and Implementation of an Unconditional Income*, Bristol: Policy Press, 2018

Van Parijs, Philippe and Vanderborght, Yannick, *Basic Income: A Radical Proposal for a Free Society and a Sane Economy*, Cambridge MA: Harvard University Press, 2017

Yang, Andrew, *The War on Normal People: The Truth About America's Disappearing Jobs and Why Universal Basic Income Is Our Future*, New York: Hachette Books, 2018

The following organisations have excellent, informative websites:

The Basic Income Earth Network (BIEN), which provides an excellent history at www.basicincome.org/history/

The Citizen's Basic Income Trust (CBIT), UK: www.citizensincome.org

What You Can Do

Donate time, ideas, skills, energy and money to your local BIEN-affiliated organisation.

Become familiar with the arguments for and against basic income and have some facts and figures about your country at your fingertips.

Use narrative and personal stories, concentrating on BI's beneficial outcomes (but without exaggerating) to change people's world view about both what is and what could be.

Change their hearts and minds.

Discuss the BI idea with your family and friends.

Organise talks, discussions and debates within your own spheres of influence.

Persuade opinion-formers and policymakers.

Challenge critics.

Discuss basic income with your elected representatives, briefing them so that they are familiar with the idea and confident enough to talk about it in public. Invite them to take part in a debate about basic income. Persuade them to support the idea in their councils or parliaments.

Remind people that BI is their stake in a compassionate society and a fairer economy, based on unconditional financial security for all on an individual basis. A BI, based on compassion, represents 'Love in Action'.

Acknowledgements

AS WITH ALL such endeavours, this book has been written on the shoulders of giants. I must thank past and present trustees of the Citizen's Basic Income Trust and the Basic Income Network Scotland. I am also grateful to the friends that I have made through BIEN for stimulating discussions over the last 37 years. The following have made valuable contributions to the text on pp 16–17: Hyosang Ahn, Sarath Davala, Ali Mutlu Köylüoglu, Télémaque Masson, Guy Standing, Toru Yamamori and Almaz Zelleke. I thank the following for reading and commenting on earlier editions and drafts of this book: John Baker, Coryn Barclay, Flo Cairns, Mike Danson, Simon Duffy, Jay Ginn, Anne Gray, Valerija Korosec, Pierre Madden and Jim Pym. I particularly thank Walter Van Trier, a fellow BIEN co-founder, for helpful guidance. Any errors are my responsibility alone. As always, I thank my family and friends for their support and patience, especially Jim and my son, Ben.

Luath Press Limited

committed to publishing well written books worth reading

LUATH PRESS takes its name from Robert Burns, whose little collie Luath (*Gael.*, swift or nimble) tripped up Jean Armour at a wedding and gave him the chance to speak to the woman who was to be his wife and the abiding love of his life. Burns called one of the 'Twa Dogs' Luath after Cuchullin's hunting dog in Ossian's *Fingal*. Luath Press was established in 1981 in the heart of Burns country, and is now based a few steps up the road from Burns' first lodgings on Edinburgh's Royal Mile. Luath offers you distinctive writing with a hint of unexpected pleasures.

Most bookshops in the UK, the US, Canada, Australia, New Zealand and parts of Europe, either carry our books in stock or can order them for you. To order direct from us, please send a £sterling cheque, postal order, international money order or your credit card details (number, address of cardholder and expiry date) to us at the address below. Please add post and packing as follows: UK – £1.00 per delivery address; overseas surface mail – £2.50 per delivery address; overseas airmail – £3.50 for the first book to each delivery address, plus £1.00 for each additional book by airmail to the same address. If your order is a gift, we will happily enclose your card or message at no extra charge.

Luath Press Limited

543/2 Castlehill
The Royal Mile
Edinburgh EH1 2ND
Scotland
Telephone: 0131 225 4326 (24 hours)
Email: sales@luath.co.uk
Website: www.luath.co.uk